THE GROWTH MINDSET

A GUIDE TO PROFESSIONAL AND PERSONAL GROWTH

BY JOSHUA MOORE AND HELEN GLASGOW

By Joshua Moore & Helen Glasgow

FREE DOWNLOAD

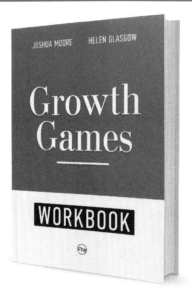

MAP YOUR GROWTH PLAN
STRAIGHT AWAY!

Sign up here to get a free copy of Growth
Games workbook and more:
www.frenchnumber.net/workbook

TABLE OF CONTENTS

Introduction

If you've picked up this book, it is more than likely that you are feeling discontented with certain elements of your current life. Whether you are unsatisfied with how your personal or professional life path is progressing, or yes, even both, this book has been written to help you re-orient your position towards personal fulfillment and professional success.

The main problem we've noticed with many self-help books of this ilk is that they immediately take on a distinct personality or character. If this personality resonates with you, then life is good and you will probably get a lot out of it. If the character of the book seems fake or impractical to you however, chances are you won't even get past the first 15 or 20 pages. And even if you are in sync with the personality of the book, there seems always to be a real disconnect when it comes to the subject of scaffolding, or applying the great stuff you learned for personal growth to your professional growth, and vice versa, if it is addressed at all.

This book will be different. WE guarantee it. How? Because we, the dynamic duo who have paired up to write this book are polar opposites when it comes to personality, life experience, motivation, individual and career focus, and how to achieve personal and professional growth. Sounds complicated? We like to think of ourselves as the perfect storm! Between the two of us and our different approaches, we pretty much cover the gamut of personal and professional growth challenges. Why? Paraphrasing the words of Jerry Maguire, from the movie of the same title, "We complete each other". My coauthor is already gagging a bit; but there is truth in these cloying words, as you will soon see. Finally, how can we be so confident in our mission? We've already been to this rodeo. We recently coauthored a book called The Emotional Intelligence Spectrum: Explore Your Emotions and Improve Your Intrapersonal Intelligence. We were so pleased by the success and positive feedback from this book that we decided to become a bit more transparent and write in a unique, back and forth manner, sharing both our commonalities, but more often and more importantly, our differences in how we perceive, approach and conquer personal and professional growth challenges. Finally, we will always leave you at the conclusion of each chapter with The Big Takeaway; combining our forces for the common good and your future personal and professional growth success! And fortunately for you, it will be all cleaned up so you won't have to witness our hair-pulling, name-calling creative process! Most of the time...

By Joshua Moore & Helen Glasgow

The Balancing Act of Personal Growth

Joshua: Helen, who you will meet on the next page, and I had our first fight when I wanted to include the word 'holistic' in the title of this book. I find oftentimes that certain words get a bad rep when they are adopted by "new age" alternative treatment types. When used as a medical term, the word 'holistic' means the treatment of the whole person, taking into consideration the effect of mental and social factors rather than just diagnosing based upon the symptoms of the disease. This would necessitate including one's environment (business or private) and status (personal or professional) when diagnosing and curing the "dis-ease" of growth challenges. All of a sudden 'holistic' is sounding a lot less "airy fairy" and a lot more necessary and practical. However, going along with the saying "A rose by any other name would still smell as sweet", I graciously conceded this point to my coauthor's wishes, modeling compromise and team playing (both excellent personal AND professional growth tools!).

This book will, thanks to our combined efforts, give you a complete, (holistic) yet practical plan; a roadmap, if you will, to self-fulfillment and/or career success. The choice is always yours to make, but as I always say, it takes balance to create an environment of optimal growth and opportunity. With that in mind, who better to pair up with in this venture than my polar opposite, a woman who has devoted her life to attaining career success, first for herself, and then "paying it forward " by sharing her wisdom and teaching others?

I have spent my life as an author, researcher, eternal student of and life coach to individuals who are in search of finding balance in their lives. I've travelled the world presenting to and training people about what I consider are the truly important and complex personal growth issues that affect each and every one of us; and I make it my personal mission to explain these topics in what I hope is a simple but practical and impactful manner. I look forward to our time together in this book, and I relish the challenges and sometimes vastly different perspective of my writing colleague Helen, who without further ado, I now introduce to you!

By Joshua Moore & Helen Glasgow

Growing Your Career to Its Maximum Potential

Helen: Gee Thanks Josh! Ok. Let's cut to the chase: my career development was (and still is) my main sphere of interests, my challenge and even my hobby. I have two Masters in Public Relations and Economics, as well as an MBA. I've managed to have a successful career in Marketing and Sales. Having reached the top of my profession, I decided to pay it forward and give a little back. I also work as a tenured teacher and trainer at corporate retreats and business conferences, specializing in "soft" business skills, including public speaking, self-marketing, corporate manipulation, and the art of persuasion and negotiation skills. Finally, as you already know, I'm also a published author.

You've heard Josh's sales pitch. Now it's my turn: Professional Growth is the KEY. In my experience, life coaches are the PROBLEM. I've been to loads, including our friend Joshua. Most of the time all I've gotten from these guys and gals is additional frustration and a sizeable dent in my purse! All I wanted was for someone to tell me how to use personal growth techniques to better myself in business. Simple, right? But all they wanted to talk about was my "feelings", my past traumas, my "miscues" and "disconnects" with peers and management, blah blah blah... And then there were the Kings and Queens of the Obvious. You know the type. They listen to you attentively, take a deep cleansing breath and then impart these pearls of wisdom: "Ummm – shouldn't a good product sell itself?" or "Why don't you figure out how to attract more customers". Ya think? Sometimes at the end of one of these sessions, I'd be sorely tempted to send them a bill for MY services, because it felt like I taught them more about how corporate business works than they taught me about scaffolding personal growth techniques around my career!

Here's my bottom line: I passionately believe that a person who works hard and builds their career should be able to learn how to apply personal growth advice to his or her career and professional life. Don't give me the talk if I can't walk it!

Josh and I have reached certain basic understandings. I know what I'm good at and he knows what he's good at. Wouldn't this be a beautiful world if everyone did what he or she was good at? But I digress. There are things Josh and I are always going disagree on. The balance thing for one. Balance makes me nervous. To me, it takes away my edge and makes me just like everyone else. I need my edge! So ok. I guess you could say I'm the "yang" to Josh's "yin"...if that means my feet are firmly on the ground where I can always "yank" him back to earth if he gets too new agey!

Anyway, for the duration of this book, Joshua and I have agreed to play nice (agreed to disagree is more like it!) and hey! At least you won't have to pay the exorbitant hourly fees he usually charges for his advice. Win Win! Seriously, I'm not against coaches who recognize the specific challenges of career success and I've paired up with Joshua because he is an excellent life coach who understands the need for professional growth. We are a great team because we challenge each other's beliefs and motivate each other to come up with better and more practical advice.

Let the Growth Games begin!

Note: There is a **Growth Games workbook** that you can download at no charge to use with this book. If you have missed it in the beginning of the book we recommend that you download it before you start reading, as it will be referenced throughout this book and will serve as a concrete roadmap for your journey to personal and professional growth!

Sign up here to get a free copy of Growth Games workbook and more:
www.frenchnumber.net/workbook

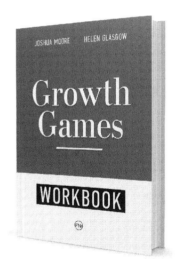

Chapter One: Planting the Seeds

In order to grow anything, you first have to prepare the "soil" in which you will be planting your seeds. This preparation includes weeding out anything that you don't want cohabitating with your seeds, and clearing out any rocks or garbage that might hinder your seeds from growing, feeding, or enriching the soil for optimum seed growth, as well as waiting for the best time of the year to plant the seeds. Proper preparation also requires knowledge gained from both the trials and the triumphs of the past; a reality check of the environment you are about to plant your seeds in; and what your future goals are for the seeds you plant today.

Preparing your Emotional Soil: A happiness retrospective

Josh: If you are even thinking about personal growth, then chances are you are about to do just that. So why not prepare your "Emotional Soil" to ensure the smoothest growth process possible and, ultimately, the best results?

I am a huge fan of locating and identifying the bottom line. I truly believe it makes the potentially complicated process of personal growth present itself in much simpler terms. In keeping with that theory, I am convinced that personal growth challenges are the result of an individual's desire to be happy; and to stay happy, by finding their own unique balance.

Easy for me to say! But how do we accomplish this? And, at this juncture, how do we prepare ourselves emotionally, to be open and ready for these changes?

The first step is to figure out how you feel at this very moment in time. If you're not at all sure, and most people searching for personal growth aren't, there are numerous personality tests that you can take free of charge online to help you determine exactly who you currently are. One of the most popular is the Myers Briggs test, which is often used in business settings to help individuals understand how they get along with others and their strengths and weaknesses. If this resonates with you, by all means utilize it! It has a proven track record and is very thorough. If, like myself, you find it all a bit complicated and detail oriented, you could always use the four Emotional Intelligence Positions from our last book The Emotional Intelligence Spectrum. These points fall in various positions on the Emotional Intelligence spectrum and are pretty descriptive of how you might be currently feeling. EU, or Emotionally Unavailable, is pretty self-explanatory. For any number of reasons, an individual who has no idea how he feels or how anyone around him feels is Emotionally Unavailable. This would be considered the low point on the EI spectrum, or to be more optimistic, the starting point. EE, or Emotional

Enlightenment, conversely, would be the mecca, or high point of the EI spectrum. It represents an ideal state of Emotional Intelligence, where the emotions of self and others are completely available, controllable, transparent, and able to interconnect with one another through an effortless flow. ee, or an Emotional Empath, is anyone who is able to discern the feelings of others to a point where it almost appears they are obsessed and hypervigilant about them. Ironically, this leaves them emotionally depleted and unable or unwilling to identify what they are feeling, except for seemingly unsourced anxiety, resentment and rage. Finally, II: one who is Id Intelligent, or as I like to think of it , "Id's all about me!", is represented by the individual who is absolutely in tune with her feelings to the exclusion of all others. Yet, despite this self-centered approach, the II person still feels empty, hurt and frustrated. If you are a visual thinker, we assigned different trees to these emotional intelligence points. EU was a dead tree, EE was a willow, ee was a tree covered in vines and stunted by bigger trees and parasitic insects and animals, and II was a lone pine tree.

Note: The ideal in terms of emotional intelligence is to be striving always towards Emotional Enlightenment, as that is the optimal position for balance and happiness.

Now that you have a basic idea of how you currently feel, you are ready to conduct the happiness retrospective which will identify when you've felt happy in the past, what makes you happy now and what you envision would make you happy in the future. Happiness is one of the strongest indicators of successful personal growth. Never underestimate the power of happiness.

The Happiness Retrospective (please refer to your **Growth Games workbook**, where you will find a copy of this to take notes on)
  • When in the past were you at your happiest?
        Why was this?
        Who was involved?
        Why did it end?
  • What currently makes you happy?
        Why is this?
        Who is involved?
        What could make it end?
  • When you plan for the future, what do you think would make you happy?
        Why would this make you happy?
        Who would be involved? (this can include people already in your life or the type of people you wish were in your life)
        What would you do to ensure it wouldn't end?

This simple, but revealing inventory of the happiness factor you've experienced throughout your lifetime should give you lots of insight about what you are primarily looking for in your future

By Joshua Moore & Helen Glasgow

personal growth journey. You know who you are and how you feel in this moment in time. You also know what has made you happy in the past, what makes you happy now and what type of growth process would make you happy in the future. Finally, you've begun a preliminary investigation of why the happiness and growth you desire could or already has been impacted or ended.

Simple action steps. Profound results. Win Win, as a friend of mine might say!

Be Your Own Best Business Project: Investing in your present and future personal growth

Helen: While I appreciate Joshua's "keep it simple" approach, I still feel the need to focus even more on the end goal, how fast it can be achieved and most importantly what the immediate as well as projected value of this growth project will be for you.

With that said, I want you to view yourself as a product you've been assigned to market in the best possible light. I also want you to list your professional growth goals as potential improvements to or benefits of this "product". Finally, just as you would have to when marketing any product, I want you to justify why you and others should invest in this product and show current and projected value. I've provided a basic business plan template for you to fill out and use throughout your professional growth process (please refer to your **Growth Games workbook**, where you will find a copy of this you can take notes on).

My Professional Growth Business Plan

Who am I In Business Today?
Career Strengths:

Career Weaknesses:

What Makes Me Unique?

Who Are My Professional Competitors?

Who Are My Professional Allies?

My Big Professional Growth Idea:

Will I work Alone or With Others?

Is this a Professional Growth idea that will be designed only to advance my career or will it also benefit and provide services for others?

How will this professional growth enhance my career strengths?

How will this professional growth improve my career weaknesses?

Why will utilizing this professional growth idea convince others to invest in me?

How can I use this professional growth to streamline and focus my career goals?

Target Market and Demographics:
Who am I marketing myself to?

Where are they in their careers? How much money or time or motivation do they have to invest in me?

What are their needs, desires, and passions?

Marketing:

How will I let others know about my personal growth?

What will be the best way to market my new improved ME?

Value:

What immediate value can I place on professional growth?

What have my competitors done as far as professional growth? What value have they gained?

How much value do I envision gaining in 6 months? A year? 5 years? What does this value look like?

Where do I ultimately see myself if my professional growth is a success?

If you are, like me, more at home thinking in terms of strategy and goals rather than finding some elusive balance or happiness, this business plan exercise should be very effective in pinpointing how you want to accomplish professional growth. I don't know about you, but my happiness factor soars when I am successful in my career and I feel like I could balance on the top of the world!

The Big Takeaway:

After reviewing each other's advice and action steps for this chapter about preparing for personal and/or professional growth, here are the 3 primary ideas we think are the most important for your future happiness and success:

- Know Where You're Starting From

    Whether your ultimate goal is to be happy and/or successful in business and/or life, it is imperative to take an accurate personal audit and establish a baseline to work from.

- Identify Your Positive Points Without Forgetting What Could Get in Your Way

    If you prefer to focus on the happiness factor then do it, but also identify what could impact or prevent that happiness. If you like strengths and weaknesses, make sure you identify and keep an eye on both.

- Envision, or Be a Visionary, but Place Yourself in the Future

    If you are comfortable with envisioning your future, guide yourself there and take the time to see every detail of how life will be after growth. If you feel you are too practical for daydreams, be, like so many highly successful entrepreneurs throughout history, a true visionary. Plot and plan your growth plan, mapping out every move and leaving nothing to chance.

Chapter Two: How Changing Your World View Affects Growth

Just as a seed cannot possibly germinate and sprout in the airless, dark little packet you purchased it in, YOU cannot experience even the beginnings of personal and/or professional growth in a vacuum. In other words, you have to take into consideration the world around you, how you view it and where you believe you fit into it.

How You Perceive the World and What It Gives Back To You

Josh: Smile and the world smiles with you; What you see is what you get; Like attracts like; Be the World you Want to See. The platitudes are endless and eternal. The sentiment may at first glance seem over simplistic and clichéd. Yet, entire fortunes have been built on this optimistic theory that if you simply put on your rose colored glasses, slap on a happy grin and smell the petunias, life will give you "The Secret" and your wildest desires will become manifest. Not surprisingly, there has been quite a backlash to certain popular books touting this sort of advice: How can you tell a starving child or a terminally ill person that if they had simply adjusted their "bad" attitude, incontro none of this would have befallen them?

This is where I believe balance comes in. Yes; bad things happen to good people. That is an incontrovertible fact. Everyone on this planet has good and bad times. I suggest it is how you react in both of these situations that determines consistent overall happiness and the ability to experience personal growth. The most important thing to remember whether you are in the depths of despair or the throes of ecstasy is not to get locked into that state. Once you are at a standstill, literally, physically, mentally or spiritually; there can be no movement. And where there is no movement, there most certainly is no growth.

Let me unpack that last statement. Isn't the goal of personal growth consistent happiness and success? Sure it is, but the catch is sustainability. Say, unfortunately, you find yourself in a bad space; the worst thing you can do is stay still. Now the classic kneejerk reaction to a negative experience is to become angry, overwhelmed, depressed, anxious, bitter and resentful of anyone who seems to be happier than you are. While these reactions are never pleasant for the participant, never mind those around them, they are a natural and organic attempt to shift up and out of the current situation, and believe it or not, preferable to just shutting down. However, these reactions expend a ton of energy, and fuel more and more negativity; coloring everything and everyone in one's immediate world view with the same muddy brush. Who could possibly find the space or motivation to foster personal growth in this environment? What if, instead, you took the same amount of energy (finding the positive light in a negative space takes an enormous amount of energy too) and started identifying good things in your life, despite the current problem? The interesting difference in taking this perspective is that even though the energy expended is approximately the same, the negative reaction just keeps refueling itself, but the positive reaction, reveals openings and opportunities for a better outcome. Allowing yourself to see the good in the world almost magically creates clear spaces where you can begin to grow again!

Conversely, say you hit the personal growth jackpot and your world suddenly becomes a mecca of joy and self-fulfillment. Should you hit the cosmic brakes and hold on for all you're worth? Absolutely not! This state of insane happiness can't be sustained any more than abject despair. It is when we are happiest that we need to be our most compassionate, humble and empathic. If we just focus on our good fortune, we become selfish, arrogant and, you guessed it...vulnerable to a tumble down the personal and/or professional growth slope.

Which brings me back to balance. Personal and professional growth is a worthy and, I believe, necessary goal for everyone, but once it is achieved it needs to be sustained. Sustainability is achievable through balance, and balance requires being able to see and appreciate both the smooth path of the balance beam as well as the endless chasms on either side of it. That is a healthy and realistic world view. Appreciate the storms as well as the sunny days, and they will all reflect positively back on you.

By Joshua Moore & Helen Glasgow

Don't Throw Yourself Off the Career Ladder: Learning to Discern How Other People Perceive Your Success

Helen: I've just finished reading Josh's section of this chapter and I must say, I'm pleasantly surprised with the lack of magical thinking in it! With that in mind, it's my turn to apply his advice to the practicality of professional growth.

Specifically, the more successful you are at climbing the corporate ladder, the more vulnerable you become to the people under, around and even above you, who may for very good reasons be not nearly as thrilled as you are with your achievements.

Business environments have their own world view, oftentimes with very different landscapes and boundaries from personal life. Josh mentioned a world view visual of a balance beam, a horizontal path to follow with unsupported and potentially treacherous areas on either side of it. In the business world, we tip that beam on its end and add rungs to it, transforming it into a ladder. There are still unsupported areas on either side of it, as well as tiny but treacherous spaces between the rungs; spaces our competition may opportunistically use to grab us by the ankles in an attempt to knock us off or make us slip. Worse still, we may imagine those grasping hands shaking the ladder because of our own lack of confidence and feelings of inadequacy.

Let me share a short story to illustrate the above. Early on in my career, I was promoted to Public Relations director of a large advertising firm. I was the youngest in the department by a good 10 to 15 years! I began to self-sabotage, worrying that my colleagues must be gossiping about my lack of experience and consequential lack of qualifications to be director. Working in a self-created vacuum, I didn't dare ask for any advice or help, figuring that would only prove my inability to lead, and I progressively sunk deeper and deeper into a state of anxiety that bled over into my personal life, resulting in sleeplessness and less and less confidence. Eventually I resigned in order to escape this shameful experience.

Now I was not then, nor am I now naïve enough to think that there wasn't some basis in reality of my fear that my colleagues were resentful of my success. Older, and wiser now, I recognize that the more successful you are in a competitive work environment, the more your work colleagues, while perhaps not gunning for your professional demise, do become more and more cognizant of your strengths and might just throw a wrench or two in your path in order to enable their own success. The bottom line is: while you need to be mindful of their feelings toward you, you can't let them get into your head!

I like what Josh said about sustainability. It's not enough to reach the top of your career ladder. You've got to be able to maintain your perch. That's where I think the ability to check your pulse as well as perform an objective reality check of your peers is critical.

I've included a self-pulse checklist as well as a peer reality checklist below. Take a moment or two and fill both out in your workbook, to see how you're feeling about the people you manage, work with and for in your career. You might get some very interesting insights from the results. At the very least you will get your detractors out of your head and safely onto a piece of paper where you can deal with them much more sensibly!

Self-Pulse Checklist

- How are you feeling?
- Why are you feeling this way?
- What have you heard?
- Are you thinking this or was it actually said?
- Is it true?
- Could it affect your career?

Peer Reality Checklist

Peer:
Position: (works under, with, or over you)
What did they say or do?
Why did they say or do it?
Is it true?
How would you feel and/or act if you were in their place?
Is it worth reacting to in a professional manner?

Can you change how they feel? Should you? Do you want to?
Could it affect your career?

Please note, the last question, i.e., the bottom line on each of these checklists is: Could it affect your career? If it can't, don't let it take up any more of your time or space in your head!

The Big Takeaway:

After reviewing each other's advice and action steps for this chapter about how your world view can affect personal and professional growth, here are the three primary ideas we believe are the most important when realigning your world view:

- Get to Know the World Around You

  Whether your goal is personal or professional growth, familiarize yourself with your surroundings. Understand the cast of characters around you, what motivates them and why. Be an observer, a listener and a participant.

- Strive for Balance and/or Sustainability

  The goal isn't a permanent state of complete happiness or success. It's finding the balance that allows you to continue to grow happily and successfully.

- Keep Other People Out of Your Head

  Don't allow what other people think or say, or worse, what you think other people think to take up space in your head. Stick to the facts that directly affect your personal and/or professional growth and discard the rest!

Chapter Three: Being Lonely and Being Alone

You may be wondering why we are devoting an entire chapter in a personal and professional growth book to loneliness and being alone. The fact is when you are alone or feeling lonely, it can result in personal or professional stagnation, deterioration and even eventual demise. So we must explore these two states, identify the differences between them, introduce the number one weapon against their potentially negative impact and provide coping tools to rise with and above them towards personal and/or professional growth.

The Journey from Feeling Lonely to the Joys of Being Alone

Josh: In this chapter, we will be dealing with two concepts that appear at first glance to be interrelated on several levels, but can actually end up on opposite ends of a spectrum. Each has negative connotations and can be confused with one another, but it is important to understand that one is a feeling that can be experienced in a multitude of locations and one is a physical state. Let's play a little word game: You can be lonely and alone. You can be alone and not lonely. You can be lonely in a crowded room, but the feeling of loneliness and the state of being alone, and it's important to make a distinction in order to allow the opportunity of other feelings to emerge in this solitary state. Chances are, you may spend quite a bit of time in your life by yourself, so it's important to understand that while you have every right to be lonely when you are alone, it is by no means the only choice!

Loneliness: At first glance loneliness doesn't seem to have much going for it. It is a reactive feeling resulting from missing something or someone. It can be a temporary feeling, experienced the first time a young child goes to school or overnight camp, or it can be a transitional feeling, when beginning a job in a new part of the country or going away to college. It can even be a seemingly permanent feeling when we lose a loved one because of a break up, divorce or death. Left to its own devices, loneliness can lead to anxiety, depression and eventual failure to thrive. Let's reflect back to the last chapter where we explored realigning our world view. When we experience loneliness in a vacuum, be it in a room by ourselves or surrounded by thousands of commuters during rush hour, it can feel like a hopeless vortex from which there is no escape. However, if we begin to take note of our surroundings and of the relationships we have had in our personal and professional lives, the gratitude we have for cherished people we have been lucky enough to know and experiences we have been fortunate enough to be a part of, loneliness can suddenly offer a thoughtful contrast and become the motivation to meet new people, try new things, create beautiful writing, songs and art, and take a fresh look at the trajectory of our lives with a new sense of urgency. Viewed under this lens, loneliness can actually foster personal and/or professional growth.

Being Alone: Many people who are not introverts think being alone is an undesirable state of being. They assume the person is alone because they have been abandoned or have somehow become lost. People end up alone for lots of reasons, some beyond their control, some chosen on purpose. It's important to remember, whether your state of "aloneness" is chosen or not, to keep other people's opinions out of your head. Pity or sympathy can erode even the best intentions of the people they are directing their reactions to. Know who you are and how you align with your world view and you will stay strong. Ironically, many types of personal and professional growth, self-help and self-improvement programs prescribe and mandate "alone time" as an integral element in healing and transformation. Bottom Line: The only person you can change is yourself – and sometimes you need to be alone to do it.

I have included a "To Do" List for those times when you are alone; whether you've chosen to be or end up there involuntarily. It includes many positive steps you can take to make the most of this time, transforming it into a productive

By Joshua Moore & Helen Glasgow

opportunity for personal and/or professional growth: (There's a copy of this list in your **Growth workbook**, if you want to take notes.)

Alone Time To Do List

Make A Schedule for Yourself. One of the hardest things to deal with when you are alone can be filling your time.

Plan Events and Activities You Look Forward To.

Make List of 5 Books you've Always Wanted to Read, 5 Movies you've Always Wanted to watch, and A Netflix Series to Binge On.

Plan Healthy Meals to Eat and Follow Through With Daily Menus

Use the Internet to Find Articles, Videos, Audio and Documentaries on Self Care.

Keep Your Living Space Clean, Uncluttered and Sensually Appealing (Fresh Flowers, Art, Color, Scent, Candles, Live plants, etc.).

Plan a Solo Vacation.

Pick Up An Old Hobby or Learn a New One.

Get Plenty of Sleep, but if You Wake Up In the Middle Of The Night, Don't Stress. Have Activities That You Enjoy and That Relax You Like Reading, Coloring or Journaling.

Create A Masterpiece: Paint a Picture, Write a Song Or a Story, Knit a Sweater, Weave a Rug. Challenge Yourself to Make Something That Will Amaze and Delight You!

Find Some Sort of Physical Activity That Burns Up Negative Energy, Calories and Anxiety. Continually Challenge Yourself to More

Strenuous Workouts. Don't Plateau or Give Up! Chart Your Progress!

Take a Day Trip by yourself and Discover a Place You've Never Been Before. Take Pictures, Pick up Souvenirs, Order Something for Lunch You've Never Tried Before.

Do you find it difficult to do things by yourself and/or for yourself? Envision planning it for someone you want to impress, and then make that person YOU!

If you haven't realized it yet, all of these suggestions have one big thing in common: They all foster self-worth and personal growth. And who knows? That new hobby or short story you ended up writing might just end up being the inspiration for a new business or positive shift in your career! Now that's a segue Helen!

By Joshua Moore & Helen Glasgow

It's Lonely at the Top

Helen: Joshua's been focusing on the difference between being lonely and being alone, and how to transform both into opportunities for personal growth, basically by giving yourself the time to get to know who you are and what makes you feel productive and happy. It's funny…There have been so many times in my career that I've dreamt of being alone for just a blessed day or two on some desert island with not a negotiation or deadline on the horizon. Being alone is a fantasy for me, but that whole lonely in a crowd of people situation? Well that really resonates with me. Actually, I'd probably be okay if I was part of the crowd. I could fly under the radar as one of the faceless masses. My problem is I've spent my whole business life trying to stand OUT from the crowd. Striving to be different, better, noticed and remembered. As a result I've been picked out of the crowd and accelerated higher and higher above it, until there I was: lonely at the top. And yes, there have always been other people at my level and at least one above me, but up there where the air is thinner and thinner, you're not exactly surrounded with a ready-made support system. Lots of people just below you are busy shaking that ladder like I talked about earlier, and the folks up at the top with me, well they're just as busy as I am holding on for dear life but never letting anyone see them sweat, and glancing sideways at each other wondering who's going to end up wanting the same prize next.

I'm not telling you this so you'll feel bad for me. Please! I've wanted to be where I am as long as I can remember: the view is astounding and the rewards are huge. Why would I devote my "free" time teaching and training people how to work their own way up those slippery rungs if I didn't love it myself? Nope; this is just the cautionary section of the fairy tale. It's not always easy being the one who everyone figures is such a killer they don't have feelings or ever have a bad day or might even make a mistake and need a little help.

I don't mean to sound resentful, but it's common knowledge that we are taught from the time we are kids to support and protect the weak ones. My question is if we always make sure the load is feather light for our more fragile friends, who's left to support the most ambitious and hard working of us? You know – the ones with the world on our shoulders? I sometimes think it never crosses anyone's mind to even imagine for a second how heavy our loads are!

I'll give you an example: A couple of years ago I accidentally bumped into a guy I know who's a top manager of a large Gaz Corporation and who was dealing with spine trauma in a rehabilitation center. So here he is, recuperating from major surgery; in a lot of pain, and this guy is still in a great mood with a smile on his face! So I figured, what the hell, and I asked him how did he do it? His reply? "If I don't cheer myself up every second then who will? Doctors? Friends? Tropical sun? Alcohol? You maybe?" He laughed and then got serious for a moment. "I can only carry on by constantly supporting myself. My mantra? 'You will manage. You WILL'."

So here's this top leader in his industry, with all the power and money in the world. But at the end of the day, he is a one-man support system. He knows the alternative is himself into a wheelchair. So he schedules precious time off and takes care of business...so he can continue to Take Care of Business!

Joshua and I have argued at great length about the value of showing your pain in the moment. I am adamant that unpacking your frailties for everyone to feast upon is completely inappropriate for the competitive work environment. We have come to an uneasy compromise: As long as you are aware of your pain, and don't deny it to yourself, which means you keep your intention to take care of it ASAP, keep up the cheerful outlook. What no one else may ever figure out is that you're multitasking in the best possible way: That cheerful outlook represents your own inner cheer LEADER; chasing away your darker thoughts with a wave of her pon pons.

What are my biggest tools when fighting professional loneliness or personal pain? Number one is Self-Care. I'm talking sense of urgency, number one priority self-care. If I wait for some down time when I can be alone with my feelings, there will be nothing left but some teeth and a hank of hair! You need to schedule self-care into your daily routine. Comb your hair, drink that first cup of coffee and do some yoga! Take that meeting, reconfigure your next two interviews and get that deep tissue massage! Work on your presentation notes, eat lunch at your desk, and head out for a run! You get the picture.

The other major weapon against professional burnout is Resilience. Josh and I talked about resilience in The Emotional Intelligence Spectrum. We said that Presence, or the ability to understand how you are feeling in the moment, plus Possibility, or being able to recognize an opportunity for growth, equals Resilience. Resiliency is the single most powerful weapon when fighting personal pain or feelings of loneliness or inadequacy. Resiliency gives you the strength to fight back. Resiliency gives you the ability to bounce back from bad experiences with a new vigor and energy. Resilience is your very essence, saying, NO. This is not how this story ends. I can choose to acknowledge my feelings, reset my attitude and expectations to possibility and reposition my professional growth compass to success and self-fulfillment!

The Big Takeaway:

After reviewing each other's advice and action steps for this chapter about loneliness, being alone and finding opportunity in both for personal and/or professional growth, here are the 3 primary ideas we believe are the most important to remember:

- Loneliness and Being Alone

  Understand what each of them are, how they affect you personally, what the difference is between them and how you can find opportunity in both for personal and/or professional growth by realigning world view.

- Self-Care

  Understand how self-care can be the gateway to personal growth as well as a necessity to ward off negative feelings, pain and burnout. Learn how to make time for it and/or how to schedule it into your daily routine.

- Resilience

  Remember: Presence plus Possibility = Resilience. Resiliency gives you the power to fight back and opens up opportunities for personal and/or professional growth.

Chapter Four: How Personality Affects Growth

Our personalities reflect not only who we are, but also our strengths and weaknesses. They often orchestrate how we will react to the random challenges of life and understanding them is an integral building block to the foundation of personal and/or professional growth.

The Big Five

Joshua: When it comes to defining personality and its integral characteristics, there are many different models to choose from. For the sake of brevity and clarity, I've chosen to utilize The Five Factor Model of Personality in our personal and/or professional growth work.

The Five Factor Model is constructed on the theory that when we are born and as we begin to develop as small children, we display one of five general personality characteristics. They are:

Openness to Experience: Characterized by imagination and insight, people who display openness to experience often have a broad range of interests, tend to be adventurous and employ creativity in all their ventures.

Conscientiousness: Characterized by a high level of thoughtfulness, people who display conscientiousness often model good impulse control, behave in a goal-directed manner and are organized and detail-oriented.

Extraversion: Characterized by emotional expressiveness, and the need to interact with others in order to energize, people who display Extraversion often are excitable, talkative, and flourish on teams and in groups.

Agreeableness: Characterized by kindness and a trusting nature, people who display Agreeableness are often altruistic, affectionate, cooperative and model prosocial behavior.

Neuroticism: Characterized by sadness and irritability, people who display Neuroticism are often prone to mood swings, anxiety and emotional instability.

An easy way to remember these 5 personality factors is to think of the word OCEAN.[1]

Besides its ease of comprehension and utility, this model has also proven to be remarkably universal in its scope. Research has been conducted around the world in many different cultures, and time and time again, the participants demonstrate one or more of these five factors. There are even people who believe this model may have biological origins, theorizing that these specific personality traits developed in human beings as those most successful to the survival and evolution of the species.

With that in mind, it makes sense that expending

---

[1] Ocean Model is developed by a group of researchers. I strongly recommend you to learn more about it at least with the help of this Wikipedia article
https://en.wikipedia.org/wiki/Big_Five_personality_traits

time and energy trying to change these integral traits of our personality, literally our essence, would be futile. At the same time, I believe it is critical that we recognize these factors in ourselves and the potential input they could have on our behavior without using them as an excuse for negative reactions or the inability to grow and change. Just because we may be predisposed to Neuroticism doesn't mean we get a free pass on the pursuit of happiness and get to spend our lives being miserable and stressed out. Rather, we should recognize these tendencies in ourselves, work on developing resiliency and focus on growth opportunities that resonate with us while being appropriate to our natural strengths and weaknesses.

In the same vein, anyone can, through the random challenges of life, be struck with depression, anxiety or physical limitations. It is who we are and how we cope that will determine what we will do to combat these "dis-eases". If we observe a person whose personality displays Extraversion and another whose personality displays Conscientiousness, and both have been diagnosed with depression, they will most likely find very different methods to alleviate their symptoms. Knowing who you are, and the general factor of your personality will enable you to identify your strengths and weaknesses and manage both when finding opportunities for personal and/or professional growth. And it is often when we are in some form of crisis that these growth opportunities become apparent. It

45

is a well-known fact that the two Chinese symbols for the word crisis are the ones meaning Danger and Opportunity!

Speaking of Strengths and Weaknesses...there are lots of schools of thought out there that believe Strengths should basically be taken for granted, as they are already, by their very nature, so well developed in us; and much more focus should be put on our Weaknesses, using up our precious resources to transform them into Strengths or eliminate them completely. This is a mistake. Our Strengths and Weaknesses are ALL part of who we are. Strengths are our gifts and need to be nourished and sharpened as they are our most powerful tools for potential growth. Weaknesses are our cautionary tales, reminding us that we are all vulnerable and they remind us to be humble and empathic (more on empathy in your personal and professional life in my book "**I Am An Empath Empaths Survival Guide: For Empathic and Highly Sensitive People**").

It all comes back to Balance. Balance is integral to sustainability and without weaknesses to counterbalance our strengths, there is neither.

Balance Makes You Average!

Helen: Ooh Josh! You had me until the balance bit! Now I have to scream it from the rooftops. When you are talking about the specifics of becoming a successful top manager in business, I will always maintain that balance is bad. You need to take that primary personality factor that makes you who you are and you need to sharpen it and polish it and make it stronger and brighter until EVERYONE sees that you are different. You are special and you are deserving of being picked out of the crowd and promoted to the top. I only wish there was a magic potion you could drink to get rid of weaknesses, but there isn't. So we have to very quietly, and privately acknowledge that we have weaknesses and manage them to an acceptable level so they don't get in the way of our trajectory to success. No one else needs to know about them! They are our little secrets...

Enough about weakness. It's time to talk about our professional superpowers! Let's take Spiderman as an example: He can make super strong webs spin out of his hands, using them to climb buildings and catch bad guys. Now if Spiderman spent all of his time trying to balance out his weaknesses, say trying to be a better cook (I'm just betting this guy is no culinary genius) or taking piano lessons (wouldn't his hands stick to the keys?) what would happen to his superpowers? Do you really think he'd be as successful or self-fulfilled if he had balanced AVERAGE abilities at spinning those webs and could only climb trees and catch cats? I rest my case.

Seriously, if I'm an introverted person who is gifted at analytical skills, that doesn't mean I can (or should!) change my basic personality to extraversion and suddenly become the next media star stock analyst, appearing on TV and podcasts across the globe and advising the rich and famous how to invest their millions. What I CAN do is focus on my analytical skills, honing them and becoming more and more respected in my field until I have earned a reputation for being the best, so that extraverted Wall Street celebrities seek me out and pay me handsomely for my gifts. I can also work on identifying compensatory skills that are appropriate to my personality. Instead of throwing myself into the nightmare spotlight of public speaking, I might take a course on effective communication using phones or Skype; learning skills that will help me overcome my dislike of talking rather than forcing me into an overwhelming situation. I need to know my limits. And I need to only expend as much energy and time as is absolutely necessary on compensating for my weaknesses.

Take a moment or two to think about your professional superpowers! And yes, always know your personal kryptonite too, but don't waste time, money and energy trying to eliminate your weaknesses. If you're allergic to scallops, it doesn't matter what you do. It's not going to change. Eat one and you're a goner.

Josh: Can I just mention, that if you think about it,

Helen and I, in very different ways, are saying the EXACT same thing?
Helen: Whatever…

The Big Takeaway:

After reviewing each other's knowledge and experience for this chapter about personality factors, their strengths and weaknesses, and how they both affect growth opportunities, here are the 3 primary ideas we believe are the most integral to personal and/or professional growth:

- Identify the Primary Factor of Your Personality

    Using the Five Factor Model of Personality, identify which of them most closely describes you and become familiar with its characteristics, strengths and weaknesses.

- Strengths

    Identify your strengths and treat them like gifts or superpowers. Nurture, sharpen, and polish them so that they are available and accessible as you pursue personal and/or professional growth opportunities.

- Weaknesses

    Acknowledge that you have weaknesses (everyone does!) and be mindful of them so that they can't cause roadblocks to growth opportunities. Don't waste time trying to transform them into strengths. Don't waste more time trying to eliminate them. Learn to live with them, privately, graciously and humbly.

Chapter Five: Identifying Growth Opportunity Support Systems

Finding your Tribe

Josh: We've already established that your emotional environment plays an important part when "planting the seeds" of personal and/or professional growth. We've also acknowledged that growth is impossible in a vacuum, and that we need to interact with the world around us in order to flourish. This chapter takes these conclusions and expands upon them to the next logical step: The need to find your tribe.

If you are one of the lucky ones, you have already established yourself within a group of like-minded individuals who collectively form a tribe. I say lucky, because the feelings of belonging and being understood and supported and encouraged to change and grow are the precious gifts you will give and receive if you have truly found your tribe. Congratulations!

But what if you haven't found your tribe? How do you go about accomplishing this? And once you find this elusive but necessary group, what are the membership requirements? And what are the membership benefits? These are all good questions. Let's start figuring it all out.

First of all no matter who you are, everyone has many years of unique experience, positive and negative, nurturing and traumatic in the art of being a tribe member. It's called growing up! Be it navigating the hierarchy of your birth order, learning the ropes in your foster or adoptive family, gaining fluency in the special rituals and language of adolescence, or jumping through the hoops of your first job, you've learned how to be a member, voluntarily or enforced, of many different groups.

As positive or negative as those experiences may have been, they are all valid experiences! The even better news is that when you set off to find your tribe, you get to choose whether or not you want to belong. That choosing is based on how much you have in common with the tribe. Tribes are forged and formed for many different reasons, but they primarily exist because of a common passion or goal. How much easier it will be to face the challenges of growth opportunities once you have identified kindred spirits facing similar challenges?

Once you have identified your primary growth goals, you then need to seek out other individuals with similar needs and desires. Depending on the type of growth opportunity you are pursuing, these tribes may be educational, professional, focused on special interest, or event based. They may be volunteer associations or think tanks, politically motivated or environmentally conscious. They may be charitable or for profit. The options are endless but the one thing they will all have in common are that they exist to enable individuals to meet and work together for

a common goal.
And what are the benefits of tribal membership?

- Lowering your risk and fear of rejection – Rejection in any form is a humiliating and demoralizing experience. Whether it's relational, situational or transitional doesn't really matter in the long run, because all rejection feels like a personal affront – even when it's "just business". We can be rejected for our ideas, our differences, our inability to sway the majority, etc. When, however, you are part of a tribe, magically the fear and sting of rejection lose its ability to single you out. Rejection of an entire group becomes a collective setback, an irritating interruption perhaps, but instead of a perceived action of dismissal as is felt on an individual level, rejection on a group or tribal level often motivates a renewed sense of urgency, a fervent call to action and the battle cry of "we have not yet begun to fight"!

- The strength of many -- This one is a no-brainer. Nothing is more motivating than to immerse yourself in a group setting where everyone is as passionate about your growth as you are. A world is created, and an atmosphere ensues where one feels anything is possible and that someone always has your back. I once attended a wellness center to learn about alternative health treatments. It was a glorious period in my life. Another student said it felt like we were all attending Hogwarts, and she was exactly right!

- Changing perception from within: If you've never seen the classic play or movie "Twelve Angry Men", find a way to see it. The plot revolves around a murder trial that appears to be and open and shut case of guilt. Back in the deliberating room, a lone juror holds out insisting on a more thorough examination of the evidence. One by one every other juror is swayed by his arguments until, as a tribe, united by justice, they collectively change their original verdict to one of innocence. A tribe, united by a cause, even if everyone isn't initially on the same page, can act as a safe place; a laboratory for changing perception and digging deeper to find the truth of the matter. While it is true that it only takes one person to effect change, the environment that brave soul stands up in can have a real impact on his or her ability to begin to persuade others to see the light.

The following is an action plan to help you find

By Joshua Moore & Helen Glasgow

your tribe. It's also in your **Growth Games workbook**, so you can make notes.

An Action Plan to Find your Tribe

MISSION STATEMENT: This should include your personal/professional growth goal(s) and explain why you are looking for like-minded individuals, teams, groups, clubs or organizations to support your mission)

OBJECTIVES	ACTIONS
Who Am I looking for?	Determine your audience
What type of group Are They?	Determine Desired Type of Group
Where Can I Find Them?	Find Sources, such as the Internet
How Can I Become a Member?	Requirements, Registration, etc
How Will They Help Me?	Research What They've Accomplished
What Can I Offer Them?	Make sure your goals align

This sort of action plan may far exceed what you need to gather a few like-minded souls together to share your personal/professional growth goals, but I've purposefully made it this way so that you can explore your desire for growth and discover more specific information about how you will accomplish this as you flesh out the details of your unique challenge with concrete inquiries and detailed actions designed to resolve them.

56

By Joshua Moore & Helen Glasgow

Networking vs. Collaboration

Helen: Joshua! I am so impressed! Objectives and action plans! I might just have to steal this for my next seminar. See folks, this is what I'm talking about: personal and professional growth advice that moves beyond theory and into the realm of reality.

Continuing in this productive direction I would like to share my thoughts about Networking, or how people think they are going to make solid, valuable contacts (tribes if you will) in their business lives. How can I put this? To me, Networking is a dead end. Sorry to shock you, but even though I can already hear the collective feet of business schools chasing me down to shoot me in the head for this, I think Networking is all about collecting business cards from potential contacts like a kid collects trading cards for his favorite sports team. All you end up with is a temporary feeling that you're actually participating in the game when in reality you've just got a purse full of paper and a fist full of dreams. As one of my MBA classmates once said, and by the way, he was a fantastic networker, it's one thing to get people's contacts and exchange calls, and another to actually get them to do something for you. Something with real value!

So my advice is to forget networking. Instead, I urge you to begin collaborating. What's the difference? Think of the phrase Walk the Talk. Networking is basically a lot of promises, lots of talk. Collaboration on the other hand is the real deal; The Walk, if you will. No one goes to the bar for a free happy hour and ends up collaborating with people. Let me explain –

When you collaborate with someone, there is always a reason behind it, as well as mutual benefits for both parties if the collaboration is a success. Collaboration is actionable.

Here's an example of when collaboration becomes useful: In business, the closer you get to the top, the more your colleagues will play what I like to call The Scapegoating Game, or Let's Find and Target a Victim. This is how it works. The Big Boss enters a top managerial meeting with the goal of finding a victim to take the blame for a failure. You know you don't want it to be you, but you also notice that often other "helpful" people will assist the Big Boss in designating the victim, and uh oh! They're looking at you! Often one "nice" colleague will initiate the witch-hunt and soon the rest of the managers join in the fun. If you're the target, they'll insist "it's nothing personal" or "nothing against you". Translation: Please God let it be anybody but me! This is when collaboration can save the day. All you need is one or two people (think back to Joshua's 12 Angry Men scenario) who can divert the unwelcome attention off of you and back to constructively discussing the original problem, along with possible solutions. The victim has been spared and the responsibility is back on the rightful parties.

So how do you actually form collaborations? Take the opportunity to lead by example. If you

By Joshua Moore & Helen Glasgow

see a colleague being targeted for victim of the day, stand up for him (even and especially if you hate him). Fight FOR your enemies; not AGAINST them, and before you know it you will notice meetings are less adversarial, more productive and there's less infighting. And it's all due to your amazing and "selfless" teamwork. Guess who smells like a rose?

Collaboration is also useful when you have a strength that can combat a colleague's weakness. I knew a brilliant coworker who was a Production Director and a gifted oral presenter, but whenever he was required to write an analytical report it was a shear disaster. I was shocked when I realized a director at his level couldn't begin to transfer his thoughts to paper, but there you have it. Strengths and Weaknesses. I suggested that I interview him and write down his answers in a written presentation. I earned his gratitude and gained a fierce advocate for my ideas for many years. All it took was writing a few well crafted (well, actually a few THOUSAND) bullets! So there you go. Collaboration in action.

So here's your homework for this chapter: I want you to find three real life work scenarios where you could use collaboration to save the day. Write down the situation, the people involved, who's being targeted, if anyone, who needs help, how you can help and how the collaboration will benefit each of you. Ready. Set. Go!

Find real life scenarios and construct collaboration action plans for them. (I've

---

included space in the **Growth Games workbook** for you to write everything down).

The Big Takeaway:

After reviewing each other's advice and action steps for this chapter about finding your tribe, collaboration and which is the right support system for you, here are the 3 primary ideas we believe are the most integral to personal and/or professional growth:

- Find Your Tribe

    Identify your primary growth goals and then seek and find other people who share your vision. Gain the strength of numbers and learn how to change perceptions from within the safety of a group.

- Collaborate Instead of Networking

    Walk the Talk and take the lead, identifying people who could use your help and benefit you in return.

- Remove the Target from your Back

    Whether your growth goal is personal or professional, use tribal membership and collaboration to ensure you are not rejected or targeted as a victim.

Chapter Six: The Inner Circle: Your Personal/Professional Confidants

Now that you have identified the general social circles or tribes and collaborations you need to belong to, it's time to focus on individuals who can be depended upon to accompany you on your growth journey.

Reliable People

Josh: Once you've found your tribe, it's only natural that you will gravitate towards one or two members more than the others. These are the chosen few who you resonate with on an astounding level. You may not have known each other for long, but on the subject of your shared passion, you can finish one another's sentences. Hopefully, it will soon become apparent that you can also rely on these people, and that they can rely upon you as well. Reliability is key when you are about to let go of the trapeze of your past and soar into the unknown expanse of personal and professional growth. This leap of faith is absolutely necessary to get to the next step, but it is also crucial that there is someone who you can rely on to catch you.

Your chosen tribe is an obvious go-to when searching for reliable people, but you may be fortunate enough to already have a life-long friend who will fit the bill. Best friends don't have to have everything in common with you to be reliable. They are reliable for the simple fact that they have withstood the test of time and stood by you as you weathered the many storms of life. When you think about it, isn't that last sentence a great definition of reliable? This type of reliable person may not always be part of your day-to-day life, but whenever you do make contact, it is as if you haven't missed a second together. A life-long friend like this seems always to stay in sync with you through your life journey, including when you explore personal and professional growth. They provide a great sounding board, and are always interested in what is currently motivating you. They will cheer on your successes and commiserate when you hit a roadblock. They will stand up for you with a fierce loyalty but also be honest with you if they believe you are heading in the wrong direction. You may become momentarily irritated with each other, but your differences will always be resolved because your love and need for each other will always take precedence. Having a life-long friend in your life is a testament to both of you because it proves you are both willing and able to do the work necessary to nurture and maintain such a resilient yet steadfast bond. By the way, anyone who can forge and maintain a life-long friendship is most certainly an excellent candidate to be successful in any personal and/or professional growth challenge!

There is yet another rich resource for finding reliable people in your family. Although you do not have the ability to choose them, sometimes family members can be your strongest advocates and allies when on the path to personal and professional growth. In an ideal world, your family is not only the ultimate tribe, but contains your penultimate reliable person. Notice that I've included the word 'ideal' in that sentence... Families, as you probably already know, can be tricky. The family unit is an intimate structure, with complex hierarchies, hidden rules, secret histories and assigned roles. The good news is, they know everything about you. The bad news is, they know everything about you. I don't mean to be flippant, but both of these statements are true. While there are countless examples of family members who are extraordinarily reliable to each other and genuinely practice unconditional love, there are just as many examples of well-meaning family members who fall short of these goals because of past trauma, preconceived notions of how someone is, based on the past and unhealed family rivalries or battles. Before you assign a family member as your personal growth "emergency contact", please look deep within your heart and choose wisely.

Co-Pilots

Helen: Finding professional "Co-Pilots" is the single most important thing you can do to accelerate professional growth. This is true even if you view yourself as "a lone wolf": find another wolf and form a pack!

In order to improve yourself professionally, find a close circle of people who are at the same professional level as you and as hungry for success in their fields. Be very picky. Colleagues with less experience than you will flatter your ego but they really don't have much to offer. People who are stronger than you will often feel annoyed with you if you try to meet them on their level. These people are potential mentors and need to be addressed in a different manner. They don't and won't have time for your day-to-day issues.

Your current place of business is a natural resource for finding co-pilots, but the ideal situation is when you have worked at 2 or three places, identified and maintained co-pilot relationships at each, and have several resources in which to exchange knowledge. Start with one or two people and cap it at a max of five or six. You are investing your time by sharing and you need to make sure your co-pilots also understand the value of this contribution.

If you are an extravert, a good resource for meeting co-pilots is at a conference. Share your opinions with people at the next coffee break and see how they react. Always ask yourself, "Are they really hungry for this topic or are they just posing and supporting the conversation just for the sake of it? Is he trying to show off to make connections?"

Don't be scared to give co-pilots who stop contributing to the dialogue limited information, but do it smoothly. Most will get the message and start participating again but if you completely cut them off you've lost them forever. Try to see it from their side – we're all human and life circumstances can sometimes can in the way of even the most aggressive executive!

The Big Takeaway:
After reviewing each other's advice and action steps for this chapter about finding your reliable people and co-pilots, here are the 3 primary ideas we believe are the most integral to personal and/or professional growth:

- Identify Reliable People in Your Life

    Whether specific tribal members, life-long friends or family members, identify and utilize the reliable people in your support system for personal and/or professional growth.

- Find Co-Pilots

    Identify colleagues who are at the same professional level as you and as hungry as you are to form a tight circle of knowledge and feedback.

- Form Mutually Beneficial Bonds

    Make sure the people you choose are willing to participate in a mutually beneficial relationship! Do not continue to support and carry them if they are not.

Chapter Seven: Specific Growth Goals

This chapter is designed to refocus you on your specific personal and professional growth goals by presenting different levels of goal development, which will enable you to clearly define and design your own. It will also explore how to analyze the people who will be involved in your growth development so you will know the best way to react and interact with them.

The Three Levels of Personal Growth Goals

Josh: It's one thing to say you want to participate in personal growth. It's another to actually know what this means to YOU. Often people start thinking about personal growth because they feel a vague yet persistent dissatisfaction with how their life is going. The term personal growth beckons them with a golden light promising happiness and fulfillment. But when asked what specific growth skills they want to develop they may not have a clue how to begin to define them or they may only be able to verbalize the end goal. End goals are useful, but the process of reaching them may be overwhelming.

Before we even look at the three levels of growth goals, let's see if you can verbalize your end goals. Try filling in the blanks of these statements: (I've included these statement with more space for notes in your **Growth Games workbook**)

I would be happier if I could just_____.

If I_____,
I would be more satisfied in my_____.

I need to_____ so that
_____

will happen.

Notice that these statements gradually become more detailed and specific. Don't be discouraged if you find one or more of them difficult to complete. I've offered these statements to show the need for a progressive method of planning growth goals.

I've devised three levels of growth goal development and I'd like to present each to you in an effort to offer you progressive clarity in reaching your own personal and professional growth goals.

The Inspirational Growth Statement: The definition of 'Inspirational' is that which makes you feel hopeful or encouraged. Inspirational Growth Statements are the first or baby step goals that will give you the optimistic foundation to build all of your other growth development upon. It makes sense that in order to achieve personal or professional growth, you first need to feel hopeful or encouraged about the hard work that lies ahead of you! When setting inspirational growth goals, I want you to use words like, "I believe", "I desire", and "I know" when formulating the specific goal. And always keep inspirational statements short and simple. Here are some examples of inspirational growth goals:

I believe I can lose weight because I've read about and seen the success of other people.

I desire to be happier because when I watch little children play I feel their joy and want it for myself.

I know I can quit smoking because there are so many different, proven methods on the market these days.

All of these statements are positive, definitive and have a justification included in them. They may seem simplistic, but they are designed purposely to give hope and encouragement. That is the goal of the inspirational statement. Take a few moments and practice writing inspirational growth statements in your **Growth Games workbook.**

Motivational Reward Statements: The definition of 'Motivational' is that which is designed to promote desire or willingness to do or achieve something. It is basic human nature that we become more competitive and focused on achieving our goals when a reward with intrinsic value is dangled before us. Reward systems abound in educational and training programs for this very reason. The hard part is matching the desired reward to the participant. What might be a very valuable reward to one person may hold zero interest for the next.

Luckily for the purposes of your Motivational Reward Statements, this problem becomes moot because you will be defining the motivational reward! Here are some examples of Motivational Reward Statements:

When I lose 35 pounds, I will buy shorts that go above my knees for the first time in 15 years!

When I am in a happier frame of mind, I will go back to singing in the choir!

When I've stopped smoking for 3 months, I will take up running!

All of these statements begin with "When" (not "If"!) and include an "I will" ending. It is crucial that the reward be desirable, meaningful and attainable to you. I've purposely made the price of these rewards low or free to prove that rewards need not be overly materialistic or expensive. Think of the American Express "priceless" campaign when you are coming up with your rewards. Please take a few moments and practice your own Motivational Reward Statements in your **Growth Games workbook**.

Aspirational Goals: NOW you are in much better shape to begin writing growth goals. The definition of 'aspirational' is that which focuses on achieving social or material success. Might I add here, that I think that is also a great definition for personal and/or professional growth?! These goals should be well thought out, far-reaching and detailed. Here are some examples of Aspirational Goals:

My goal is to lose weight so that I can pursue a healthier lifestyle, and explore my dream of working in the alternative health field as a massage therapist and personal life-coach. I will practice what I preach!

My goal is to be happier so that I regain the confidence I lost when I got divorced and become more involved in my church by singing in the professional gospel ensemble and touring with them! I will not waste my gifts!

My goal is to quit smoking so that I can be an active grandparent, involved with their sports teams and able to hike up a mountain or run on a beach with them. I will be an active participant in their lives!

Now think back for a moment...If I had asked you at the beginning of this chapter to write Aspirational goals, would you have been stuck for the words? That is why it is important to understand that there are levels and steps to the personal and professional growth process. When you are ready, please take some time and practice formulating your own Aspirational Goals in your **Growth Games workbook**. Remember this sentence: You need to be INSPIRED in order to MOTIVATE yourself to be ASPIRATIONAL. Have fun and dream BIG!

The Bottom Line

Helen: I don't want to invalidate what Josh has just told you. Depending on where you are in your life you may very well need to start at the Inspirational level and I wish you all the luck in the world. For my purposes however, I'm going to jump right to the Aspirational Part. In business, aspirational goals are often promotional in nature, in that you are promoting your ideas, your skills, your experience, YOU, to upper management, because your professional growth goal must always be PROMOTION! See how I did that?

When attaining this promotion goal, ask yourself who your boss will most likely promote. What type of person does he need? Then go a step further. Think about your boss's boss, the one I like to call 'The Godfather'. What does he need? What could you do to make your boss look better in The Godfather's eyes? Sometimes the quickest way to your next promotion is helping your boss get recognized by The Godfather.

Important note: Never go around your boss to get to The Godfather. This is the quickest way to get your boss to hate you forever.

To help you figure out how best to get into the mindset of your boss and his boss, I've compiled a dossier on the major "types" of bosses and what's the easiest way to score a quick win with each them as well as how to make a mortal mistake:

THE KING ON THE HILL BOSS: This man or woman has gotten to where they are by being a quiet genius at what they do. They are purposefully elusive and distant and they will only interact with others on a strict NEED TO KNOW basis. This may have nothing to do with their personality, but whether it does or doesn't, they will appear arrogant and cold. They protect themselves behind protocol and they further armour themselves by adhering to the strictest of boundaries.

Quick Win: Be the person they need with the answers they need when and where they need them. Case closed. Accept the challenge or stay away.

Mortal Mistake: Try to joke with them and get to their "just folks" side!

THE BEST FRIEND BOSS: This woman or man is gregarious, charming and has an amazing ability when talking to a roomful of people to make you feel like they are directing all their attention to you! They are detail-oriented, extraverts, have great senses of humor and people skills plus.

Quick Win: Show genuine appreciation of their golden presence without kissing their ass too obviously. They are the star; you are the appreciative audience who always gets their jokes.

Mortal Mistake: Don't even think of being funnier or cleverer than they are, especially if you are funnier or cleverer! Also, avoid divulging too much information to these folks. They are hyper vigilant and always looking for that one piece of information that will give them a solid handhold up the next mountain, and they are brilliant when it comes to getting people to spill their guts.

THE EXPLOSIVE BOSS: This lunatic has somehow risen to the top merely because EVERYONE is intimidated, no, terrified, of his or her explosive nature. They are chameleon-like in their ability to seem like everything is going well, until, like a snake they randomly strike without warning, scorching the earth and everyone on it in their immediate surroundings.

Quick Win: The less exposure; the better. Fly under the radar as much as you can, and know their enemies (fools!) so that when they are around you can take cover under the nearest desk. Pray at night for their eventual demise and scour the in-house open positions for an escape.

Mortal Mistake: Confront them. I dare you...

THE LAZY BOSS: This guy or gal has probably been demoted more than a few times in his or her life and been let go of a few different companies to boot, Yet, their superpower is that they have the singular ability to repackage themselves, and through loads of contacts who don't really know them well enough and sheer luck, manage to stay in the managerial game. They will pawn off as much work and responsibility as they can and if you are a hard worker, they will target you as their best friend.

A snapshot of them usually involves them on the phone, tilted back in their chair, with their feet on the desk. Their favorite phrase: "I don't have to look at this. I trust your work."

Quick Win: If you want their job, work as hard as you can but make sure EVERYONE knows you did it.

Mortal Mistake: If you have any masochistic tendencies or are obsessive compulsive stay clear of these types. They will work you into the ground.

THE "I STARTED FROM THE BOTTOM" BOSS: This lady or gentleman has been at the company since they were 18 years old. They started out in the mailroom or the secretarial pool and they are the experts on everything to do with how this company runs because they have literally DONE everything to make this company run! These people come in two flavors. If they are still vital members of the staff, respected by all and treasured for their wealth of knowledge, they are amazing professional resources. If they are burnt out relics leftover from the "golden" era of the company, they are irritable old gasbags to be tolerated and cared for until their retirement.

Quick Win: Show them respect and curiosity about their accomplishments and contributions and they may very well gift you with valuable advice and knowledge.

Mortal Mistake: Ridicule the way things used to be done and they will become your worst enemy.

THE MENTOR: Ding Ding Ding! You've hit the jackpot. These bosses do exist. They are motivated by inner goodness and a high moral compass and quite possibly that stint they did in the Peacecorp after college. Whatever makes them the way they are, these social entrepreneurs are only too happy to mentor, pay it forward and give back to a worthy employee. Their secret: they derive just as much pleasure from teaching as they do from leading.

Quick Win: Respect them, take the challenges they give you and come back with positive results; take what you've learned and pay it forward in your turn. Mortal

Mistake: Let them catch you trying to shake someone else off the career ladder and you'll get to meet the steely person who rose to the top despite how nice they are!

The Big Takeaway:

After reviewing each other's advice and action steps for this chapter about developing specific growth goals and analyzing the people who could impact these goals, here are the 3 primary ideas we believe are the most integral to personal and/or professional growth:

- Identify and Communicate the levels of your growth goals

  > Allow your growth goals to develop from the inspirational to the motivational until they emerge as aspirational.

- In Business, don't forget the bottom line

  > I am promotable. Therefore I am!

- Know your boss

  > If your goal is promotion, you need to know who the bosses are; how they roll and what you can do to win them over to your goal as well as what NOT to do so you don't gain a mortal work enemy.

Chapter Eight: Organizing Your Personal and Professional Growth Environment

In this chapter we use personality factors to help identify growth development methods and actions and learn how to manage for "The Big Picture".

Using the Five Factor Model to Organize Your Plan of Attack

Josh: You know, the more I collaborate with Helen, the more aggressive I find my terminology becoming! "Plan of Attack"! I think I am magnetized to these more urgent, action centric words when it comes to the practical implementation of personal growth development, because once you move beyond theory, unless you have a concrete action plan, the physical action of personal growth can become elusive and overwhelming. As I tried to combat those characteristics in the last chapter about the stages of developing growth goals, I wish to continue in the same manner in this chapter where we will set the stage for personal growth development, using the Five Factor model introduced in Chapter Four to determine the most personality appropriate actions.

Here's why you need to factor in your personality type when planning how to implement your personal growth goals: say, for example, you are a neurotic personality type who is trying to overcome an eating addiction. How well do you think you're going to do in a group situation, where one of the main focuses is based on a military style boot camp, with bulked up personal trainers barking orders and screaming at the people who are flagging to "hit the deck and give me 20?" My apologies if you are reading this and you are a neurotic personality with an eating addiction, because you are probably now having an anxiety attack! What if instead, you were enrolled in a lower key program that focused on mindfulness and alternative therapies such as light therapy, tai chi and gentle yoga? You see my point.

I am going to list all five personality factors once again and give advice and suggestions on how to pair them up with appropriate methods and activities you can utilize when implementing your personal and/or professional growth development.

Openness to Experience: Characterized by imagination and insight, people who display openness to experience often have a broad range of interests, tend to be adventurous and employ creativity in all their ventures. Appropriate methods and activities for this personality factor would include any activity that has an element of exploration, adventure or discovery to it, such as outward bound, extreme sports, ecotourism, volunteer work and travel opportunities, alternative therapies, spirituality, Shiatsu and Ayurveda practices.

Conscientiousness: Characterized by a high level of thoughtfulness, people who display conscientiousness often model good impulse control, behave in a goal-directed manner and are organized and detail-oriented. Appropriate methods and activities for this personality factor would include journaling, scheduled action plans, activities with rules, regulations and good boundaries, structured classes, homework and tests, seminars and trainings where credits and certificates are earned, training for marathons or triathlons, competitive sports, furniture making classes, cooking classes and language immersion programs.

Extraversion: Characterized by emotional expressiveness, and the need to interact with others in order to energize, people who display Extraversion often are excitable, talkative, and flourish on teams and in groups. Appropriate methods and activities for this personality factor would include: Improvisation classes, social dancing classes, standup comedy classes, cross training, boot camps, talk therapy, team sports, public speaking classes, "soft skill" business seminars, discussion groups, social activism, think tanks and blogging,

Agreeableness: Characterized by kindness and a trusting nature, people who display Agreeableness are often altruistic, affectionate, cooperative and model prosocial behavior.

Appropriate methods and activities for this personality factor would include cooperative groups and games, volunteer activities such as soup kitchens, food banks and habitat for humanity, mentoring and tutoring opportunities, team dancing such as clogging, folk or line dancing, instrumental music ensembles and acapella singing groups.

Neuroticism: Characterized by sadness and irritability, people who display Neuroticism are often prone to mood swings, anxiety and emotional instability. Appropriate methods and activities for this personality factor would include private therapy, one-on-one activities, art and music therapy, light therapy, massage to relieve stress, meditation, guided imagery, creative writing, painting, composing, photography, gentle yoga, positive thinking, Ted Talks, healing touch and Reiki.

By Joshua Moore & Helen Glasgow

Seeing the Big Picture

Helen: When you organize and manage your team of employees at work, act as if you are running a company. Too many times managers stall their own career trajectory by falling into a "cog-in-the-wheel-mentality", and ignoring The Big Picture. When you keep the company's overarching goals and missions in mind as you manage your section of it, you are automatically transported to a different level when you talk to the General Manager. Just because you're the manager of a small IT/design/call center team doesn't mean you shouldn't be well versed and ready to talk about Big Picture issues such as costs, ROI, KPI, revenue and profit growth strategies. In this case you need to "walk the talk: until people start asking your opinion and you are invited to more advanced meetings on more overarching managerial subjects.

The Big Takeaway:

After reviewing each other's advice and action steps for this chapter about organizing your personal and professional growth environments, here are the 3 primary ideas we believe are the most integral to personal and/or professional growth:

- Take your Personality Type into Account

  Match your implementation methods and activities to your personality factor and consider your strengths.

- Manage the Big Picture

  Don't fall into "cog-in-the-wheel" mentality.

- Walk The Talk

  Manage your department as if you are running the company until other people take notice, start asking for your advice and inviting you to bigger meetings.

Chapter Nine: Social and "Soft" Skills Development

Successful personal and professional growth is dependent upon your ability to access and utilize social and "soft" skills.

Playing Nice…

Josh: When embarking on any Personal or Professional Growth project, there comes a point where, in order to keep growing you need to honestly review your social skills and see how you rate. There's a reason every grade school report card you ever got had a section on it grading you on how well you "worked and played with others". It's a crucial life skill and trumps talent and brains every time when it comes to personal and professional growth implementation!

But wait. If you are supposed to be learning to assert yourself to get ahead and be satisfied and successful isn't it contradictory to be developing your "nice" skills? What would Helen say?

Well now, Helen does have a thing or two to say about "soft" skills, but let's not jump ahead of ourselves.

"Nice" skills include conflict resolution, and the ability to negotiate and control situational, relational and transitional disturbances. Conflict resolution is the ability to negotiate yourself and others through the potentially messy and damaging waters of disagreements, fights, battles and wars. It's quite a gamut and a lot of responsibility for a "nice" set of skills! As we wrote about in The Emotional Intelligence Spectrum, the ability to negotiate various disruptions is also crucial. These disruptions can be: situational, i.e., disruptions caused by an event in a specific time and/or place such as active duty in a war zone or being bullied in school; relational, i.e., having to do with other people, such as the breakup of a marriage or taking care of a loved one in hospice; or transitional, i.e., caused during a life transition such as Having a baby or a mid-life crisis. I can pretty much guarantee you have or will go through many of the disruptions listed above and I don't want to think about how much your personal and/or professional growth development might suffer if you didn't have the skills to get through them.

In I Am an Empath, I wrote about Empathic Protection, or how to negotiate relationships when you tend to be empathetic and end up worrying about how everyone else feels and sacrificing your own emotions. I also wrote about Stress and Anxiety Reduction techniques including setting emotional limits, grounding techniques to use in stressful situations and how to deal with information overload. Helen and I are devoting a chapter to empathy later in this book, but I thought these examples dovetailed nicely in my argument for the need to have excellent social skills.

I have assigned space in your Growth Games workbook to list some of the conflicts, situational, relational and transitional disturbances you might be currently grappling with. Jot them down and think up some strategies o/n you could negotiate them better in the future. Also, go on the Internet and look up grounding and other relaxation techniques. They can be a lifesaver in times of stress, positive or negative, whether dealing with conflict or implementing growth!

The Hiring Dilemma: Technical Skills or "Soft" Skills?

Helen: When hiring, there is an ongoing debate on whether the ideal job candidate should have the most technical job qualifications or be a great manager. There's lots of feedback from both sides of the argument, especially the side with the more technically proficient folks. I'm sorry to disappoint BOTH sides of the fence, but in this economy with the current level of unemployment we're seeing, the answer is BOTH! Today's corporations and businesses are in the driver's seat and they want, NO, they demand it all. So it's time to suck it up and invest in ourselves.

If you want to be taken seriously in today's job market, (and if you don't want your current position to be your last promotion!) I highly recommend the following topics to head your professional development to do list:

- Finance for the Non-Financial Manager
- The Art of Delegation
- Basic and Advanced Management
- Conflict Resolution
- Advanced Excel
- Team Management
- Marketing Basics
- Negotiation Skills
- How to Protect Yourself from Manipulation
- Advanced Power Point Presentations

But don't stop here! I've made room in your **Growth Games workbook** to list every management job in your present company as well in other companies you are interested in. Included all the skills requested and/or required on the job listing and start making plans on how you can gain these skills ASAP!

The Big Takeaway:

After reviewing each other's advice and action steps for this chapter about honing your social and "soft" skills, here are the 3 primary ideas we believe are the most integral to personal and/or professional growth:

- Understand the Necessity and Power of Social skills

  > Conflict Resolution and situational, relational and transitional disturbances cannot be resolved without excellent social skills. Social skills can also protect and ground us in times of stress.

- Managing Means People

  > You need "soft" skills to be a skilled manager.

- Arm Yourself For Today's Demanding Job Market

  > You have to have it all in today's demanding and discerning job market. Arm yourself with all the technical and "soft skills" you need to succeed.

Chapter Ten: Give until you grow!

Here we answer the question of why it is important to give.

The Healing Circle of Giving

Josh: It is one of life's more counterintuitive facts, that just when you feel at your lowest in life, through a loss event, a disappointment or a perceived failure; one of the most productive and life-affirming things you can do is to pick yourself up, change out of those dirty sweatpants, brush your teeth and go out and give to someone else. How can this be? And yet, it is. When you give of yourself, "Pay it Forward" as friend of mine likes to say, the benefits are numerous and beneficial.

- If nothing else, the act of giving momentarily shifts your attention off of you and requires you to focus on someone else's needs.
- When you give by sharing one of your strengths or "gifts", you have to identify it as such and the successful reception of this gift confirms and affirms that it truly is just that.
- When someone receives this giving time from you, chances are you will feel fulfilled and proud.

- It's an old cliché, but nonetheless true. When you give to someone less fortunate than yourself it makes you appreciate what you have.
- Giving of your time and gifts gives you renewed confidence and optimism in return.

Of course, you don't have to wait until you're in the depths of despair to give to others. I highly recommend trying to work it into your personal growth implementation lineup. Is there any one of the benefits listed above that wouldn't be beneficial to your personal growth? I didn't think so!

By Joshua Moore & Helen Glasgow

GIVE Because...

Helen: The best way to build quality relationships at work is to GIVE first and ask later. Sometimes it isn't enough just to share something, as you would in collaboration. Giving a person something really valuable without being asked for it can instill fundamental trust in you and your professional ethics. I'd never tell you to give away information or ideas that might amount to "giving away the store", BUT if you've thought it through and it's not going to bite you later, I can think of nothing more effective to help you build solid relations at work AND in your personal life, than the altruistic act of free will giving; giving something of genuine value away. The key is to mean it. You can't have any other agenda but that of starting a solid relationship based on generosity. If you can really afford to do it, my advice would be to get on with it without a moment's hesitation. How's that for counterintuitive advice Josh?

Hey, come to think of it, this book that Joshua and I have put together for you is a great example! It took us a lot of time to put it together, but we wanted to introduce ourselves and our individual styles to you before you went ahead and spent your money on our other books. We wrote this book and give away for free its eBook version with the intention of giving you value in the form of our knowledge and advice. We sincerely hope you feel like you received a good gift!

The Big Takeaway from a little chapter...

- GIVE

    Because it will make you feel good!

- GIVE SOME MORE

    Because it is personal and professional growth implementation in action!

- KEEP ON GIVING

    Because it's a great way to form fundamental trust and solid personal and professional relationships!

Chapter Eleven: Growing Toward Security and a New Comfort Zone

It may sound contradictory, but sometimes the primary goal of personal and professional growth is security and the creation of a new, genuine comfort zone where you can truly feel at home.

When Your "Comfort Zone" Becomes a Lock Down

Josh: In the Self-Improvement Business it's very common to hear from many specialists, teachers, trainers and coaches that in order to grow and improve yourself you need to leave your "comfort zone'. Personally, whenever I hear that term, a sarcastic voice in my head whispers, "Sure. Just let me enter it first!" Honestly, how many people do you know who live in a nice, smooth little comfort zone? I think the term comfort zone needs to be redefined in terms of people who are searching for growth and improvement. What we should say is "you need to leave the zone you are used to, the zone that you are presently being held prisoner in." While it is certainly true that we become accustomed to all manner of unhealthy environments, it is a misnomer to label that familiarity as "comfort". I have a real difficulty demanding that people abandon this "discomfort" zone before they understand where they are and have the inspiration and peace of mind to leave it.

For example, you cannot ask people who desire weight loss to simply stop eating and start working out like an Olympian until you've taught them to be comfortable with their current body and mindset, until they begin to love themselves. When you love someone, you will do anything to protect and care for him or her.

Once we shift the terminology from comfort zone to discomfort zone and help people understand that they've gotten used to an unacceptable environment, then the inspiration, motivation and aspirational goals can be designed and implemented. Reaching and succeeding in those goals will automatically give the participant true security in the form of improved physical and mental health, the improved potential to earn a living, form and maintain healthy relationships: the peace of mind you can only achieve when you know you are in control of your destiny. Now THAT is a true Comfort Zone, and one we all deserve and should aspire to.

By Joshua Moore & Helen Glasgow

Pyramid of Security and Success

Helen: If you have ever been at all interested in personal and/or professional growth, you've probably been exposed at some point to Maslow's Pyramid of Need, a concept and graphic illustrating from the bottom of the pyramid up: Physiological Needs, or the basics like food, water, warmth and rest; Safety Needs; Belongingness and Love needs; Esteem Needs, such as feelings of accomplishment and finally at the pinnacle, Self-Actualization, meaning the point where you've achieved your full potential.

As part of my mission to scaffold the concepts of personal growth to the specific requirements of professional growth and without further ado, I now present you with Helen's Pyramid of Security and Success!

#1
Self-Care
Your 'A' Team
Saving for Retirement
Entry Level Positions/Learn From the Bottom Up!

Let me elaborate: When you begin your career, the only thing that matters is getting that entry-level position. This is where you will be introduced to all aspects of the business you want to lead someday. If you need to be an optimist, this is where you basically get paid a bit of money to start your business education. It's a great deal when you look at it that way!

98

Once you have established yourself on a career ladder, it's time (and remember it's never too early!) to start saving for your retirement. You are no longer on the bottom rung, and from now on any move you make must be a positive one that allows you to save for the time you will no longer want, or be capable of working.

Once you are established as a manager with staff reporting to you, you need to choose you 'A' Team. This includes your direct reports, but also your professional collaborators, your co-pilots and hopefully, your mentor bosses.

When you've reached the Self-Care level of my pyramid, you probably are in desperate need of it! Upper management jobs come with awesome responsibilities, tight deadlines, long hours, endless conflict, stress and pressure to produce on command. This is where you need to plan fully scheduled time for health clubs, massage, preventative nutrition and time away. Ideally, I like to imagine that where I've positioned Self-Care on my pyramid, it can trickle down to all the levels below it as well as provide a cushy floor beneath the top level.

#1 is self-explanatory. It's where you need to be aiming for throughout your entire career. It's the top of the ladder. The views are fabulous but don't ever look down! Seriously, when you've reached #1, you need to be mindful of your hard work and good fortune. This is where you've hopefully become the ideal, mentor boss, helping others up their own ladders and pyramids!

Now I'd like to focus on professional "Comfort

Zones". Think of your work environment. Do you feel relaxed and comfy at your job, or does it supply you with emotional discomfort every single day? (Emotional Discomfort – I'm turning into Josh!). I am in total agreement with my co-author on this subject. Just as in your personal life; professional growth should direct you from the current zone of "discomfort" you are stuck in, and redirect you to a genuine comfort zone. Comfort zones in professional life usually mean financial security and stability.

In order to position yourself in a professional comfort zone you need to concentrate on two things: Reputation and Assets.

Your reputation is one of your most powerful tools to gain respect from bosses, peers and reports, as well as a powerful form of insurance to ensure future employability. It's no secret that the older you get, the more difficult it can be to find a job. It's difficult for everyone but having a reputation for being flexible, innovative, keeping up with the latest technology and fostering mentor relationships with younger employees can go a long way to overcoming this challenge.

The following exercise will help you honestly evaluate your business reputation, and if you find it lacking in certain areas, provide a call to action to make immediate amends in the form of professional growth implementation. I've included this exercise in your **Growth Games workbook** if you want to make notes.

Reputation Review

What Do You Think your Business Reputation is?

What Did Your Last Annual Review Say?

What Do You Think your Colleagues Say About you?

What Do You Think your Reports Say About You?

What Do your Trusted Collaborators Say About You?

What Do your Trusted Co-Pilots Say About You?

What Do your Friends Say About You Professionally?

What Does your Family Say About You Professionally?

Do You Have A Reputation in your Industry?

What are your Professional Strengths? Weaknesses?

What Will You do to Improve your Reputation?

How Will You Market Your Reputation to Prospective Employers?

When it comes to asset management, no matter how young you were when you began saving, it will never seem that you started early enough! With that said, it's more important to start saving, no matter what your age is. Start NOW! I promise I will write a book specifically geared to the challenge of catching up on your retirement savings, but until then I want you to come up with a solid Plan B if you should suddenly lose your current job. What else could you do? Are there other careers that your experience and skill sets could transfer to? I've added space in your **Growth Games workbook** for your to map out your prospects, listing your skills and experience so you can view them all in one place, think about them, sleep on them and start making contingency plans, just in case... Meanwhile, I'll be writing that book!

The Big Takeaway:

After reviewing each other's advice and action steps for this chapter about Security and Comfort Zones, here are the 3 primary ideas we believe are the most integral to personal and/or professional growth:

- What "Comfort Zone" Really Means

    What all the specialists are really saying when they suggest leaving your comfort zone, is to leave the zone of "discomfort" you have become accustomed and locked into.

- Helen's Pyramid to Security and Success

    Traversing the steps to Job/Life Security and Professional Success.

- Reputation and Assets

    The two most powerful tools against unemployment and financial decline.

Chapter Twelve: Utilizing Empathy to Implement Growth

Empathy, or the ability to understand and experience other people's emotions, is often viewed as a double-edged sword. When one is an Empath as discussed in **The EI Spectrum**, and Joshua's book **I Am an Empath**, the "gift" of empathy is so highly developed that they may sacrifice their own feelings, needs and desires, consumed by the feelings, needs and desires of others. But when empathy is tempered by self-awareness and appropriate boundaries, it can become an insightful, intuitive tool when implementing personal and professional growth goals.

Interacting with Others through Empathic Practice

Josh: Whether you are intimately familiar with you empathic side or you never really gave it much thought, empathy, or the lack thereof has a definite impact on personal and professional growth implementation. I will refer once again to the "there is no growth in a vacuum" statement. Both personal and professional growth implementation need human interaction in order to flourish. It's kind of like the tree falling in the forest conundrum... If you're out there all personally grown and enlightened, but you don't interact with anyone... have you really grown?

So, if you are empathic by nature, i.e., very comfortable putting yourself in other's shoes and have a highly tuned radar for the feelings of others, you will already have the ability to innately sense how to interact with others in tribes, collaborations, through conflict resolution and the various disturbances that crop up during personal and professional growth development. Empaths need to take care that others do not overshadow their own growth goals; to remain attuned but balanced and grounded.

If, however empathy is not among your natural gifts, you can develop it by being mindful when interacting with others that they have feelings, needs and desires as passionate as your own. You may need to practice, learning techniques such as Active Listening, or imagining yourself in your adversaries' place. Guided imagery and role-playing are also helpful when trying to tap into your empathic side.

Be the Mentor Boss You Wish You Had

Helen: Remember when I profiled some general types of bosses earlier in this book? Well, when you think of empathic practice in the workplace, think of the Mentor Boss. Obviously, in the dog eat dog world of competitive business practices, you can't walk around the office with your heart on your sleeve, weeping and gnashing your teeth for all those suffering from emotional distress, BUT you can thoughtfully and genuinely think about where your colleagues as well as your competition is coming from. I've used the words thoughtful and genuine to verbally underscore that this can't be a facile or fake action. This is no place for hidden agendas and duplicity. But, if you are serious, it is the place to polish your reputation and show yourself in your best light to your boss, current and future.

So be the Mentor Boss you've always wanted. Manage empathically; keep your ear to the office floor and stay abreast of what's going on in your colleagues' personal and professional lives. If it's appropriate, this is great time to give without strings, to listen and to advise. If you are in competition for a project or a promotion, take the time to get to know your competition a little better if you can. Care about them as people, and keep petty jealousies and rivalries in you briefcase. It won't cost you much and the least that will happen is you'll be a better person for it, which in terms of personal and professional growth is no small thing.

The Big Takeaway from a little chapter...

- Empathic Practice for Growth Implementation

    Put yourself in someone else's shoes so you know where they're coming from.

- Practice Balanced Empathy

    Protect yourself from sacrificing your own growth goals.

- Be a Mentor Boss

    When you manage empathically, you gain insight, compassion and a great reputation.

Chapter Thirteen: The Pitfalls of Fulfilling the Aspirations of Others

While it is a fact that human interaction is an essential ingredient of personal and professional growth development, you must be mindful at all times of who is driving the bus. When you spend your time and energy fulfilling the aspirations of others, you may find yourself very unhappy with the journey, as well as the final destination.

Everybody's talking At Me...

Josh: In chapter three, in the section about being alone, I mentioned that sometimes people are perfectly fine being by themselves, UNTIL a well-meaning friend or family member makes some comment about how sad it is, or how brave they're being, or how hard it must be for them to be on their own. Oftentimes a casual observation like this can completely change the mind-set of the solitary person, and they begin to doubt their acceptance of the situation, becoming anxious that there is really something wrong with them. Human beings are very susceptible to the opinions of others, especially when these opinions mirror societal "norms".

Another, potentially more insidious way that people can get inside our heads and deviate our original growth goals is when a loved, respected and/or authoritarian figure in our lives assigns, suggests, demands or manipulates us into fulfilling aspirations they have chosen for us. There are many different ways this can happen. The scenarios include: A father and surgeon, who assumes from the time of his first-born son's birth, that he will follow in his footsteps and also be a surgeon; the revered acting coach who tells his young impressionable and talented student that she really isn't good enough to be a professional actor and should become a teacher; the wife who berates her happy carpenter husband for not being a good enough provider until he packs his tools and becomes a midlevel manager at a high tech corporation; the elderly mom who decides her youngest daughter should be her caretaker instead of perusing her journalism dream job across the country. I have to stop here. Just the act of writing these sentences makes me feel tense and resentful.

It may be the hardest thing you ever have to do, but if it takes every ounce of fortitude you have, you've got to be true to yourself and resist letting other people hijack your dreams and aspirations. No one deserves a life of quiet desperation, and yet it happens over and over again. If you are already living this sort of life, and are feeling trapped, you need to give yourself the time and opportunity to stop the wheels from endlessly turning and begin to plan an escape route. Just like any other growth goal, you need to find inspiration, be it in the form of counseling, a trusted confidant, professional life coaching or asking help from other family members. Then you need to put practical, attainable, goal-oriented motivational steps in place. Finally you need to envision and develop rich, detailed aspirational goals that you will implement and you will attain. You can't get overwhelmed by the big picture. You have to deconstruct the challenge into bite-sized steps, accomplishing one at a time and celebrate each small victory. It might take a long time to completely extricate yourself or deviate enough from the original intention to a place where you feel happy and satisfied, but that is no time at all in comparison to a life lived at the whim or dictum of another. Find your tribe, and your reliable people, share your dreams and desires and move forward.

Sticks and Stones...

Helen: If you are serious about the kind of professional growth that results in promotion after promotion in a competitive workplace, then you will need to develop a very thick skin to deflect the slings and arrows of the many "office games" your co-workers will play. One of the key problems with professional growth is that the more successful you are, the more your colleagues are going to notice and compare themselves to you. The better you are trying to be as a person and a professional, the more jealous and angry these same colleagues will become.

I've already discussed how important self-care and being your own best support system is, but it bears repeating in a different way here: You will never be good enough in the eyes of everyone at work. If your boss thinks you're professional – that's great! Will other co-workers rejoice in your good fortune? Hell no! Out will come the Microscope of Criticism and suddenly no mistake of yours will be too small to be scrutinized and paraded, complete with fireworks, for the rest of the company to see! This humiliating little game is honestly considered a professional growth tool by some, who when confronted with their dirty deed will chirp, "Nothing personal!" Have you ever noticed that as soon as someone says "nothing personal" it suddenly gets VERY PERSONAL?

So how do you develop this thick skin? The one

thing you need to remember is to stay true to your aspirations...AND ONLY YOUR OWN!

How often have you been assigned a project and you know from the get-go that it's NEVER going to be as perfect as it needs to be? Whether it's due to time constraints or tight budgets, you will not be able to deliver the envisioned result. So what should you do? You need to take yourself away, sit yourself down and make an agreement with yourself before you do another thing, to work to the best of your abilities within the framework you've been handed to a level of completeness that is satisfactory to YOU! Write it down. Date and sign it. I mean it! When the project is over, go back to these notes and this agreement, review it, deconstruct it, learn what you can from it, and MOVE ON.

This self-contract works for all sorts of challenging situations, especially ones where you are required to perform using methods and skills that are not among your strengths or gifts. Sit yourself down, be scrupulously honest with yourself and decide upon an acceptable level of success that you are confident you can attain.

I've included space in your **Growth Games workbook** to practice this essential exercise. Don't underestimate its necessity or its ability to see you through the jungle we call work.

I leave you for now, with one of those "What I say in this book, STAYS in this book" stories for your entertainment. Don't try this at home folks!

I once joined a company at the same time the new CEO did. He came in under a black cloud and was already perceived negatively by the current management team. In fact I got MY job there because one of the first things he did was fire a former Marketing Director and I was headhunted and hired as a result, and, might I add, without any knowledge of this incident. As a result, the management team viewed me as his "girl" and therefore an enemy. I really didn't want to spend months breaking the ice because of somebody else's battle so I proposed to the CEO that at the next meeting we both attended, that I make a really bad "mistake" which he would lose his mind over and read me the riot act. He agreed and we went through with our little performance. After that, the management team took me under their collective wing because of the "Big Bad CEO"!

Again, don't do this. Really...don't.

The Big Takeaway:

After reviewing each other's advice and action steps for this chapter about the pitfalls of fulfilling the aspirations of others, here are the 3 primary ideas we believe are the most integral to personal and/or professional growth:

- Don't listen to the well-intentioned.

    When it comes to personal and professional growth try to keep other people's opinions out of your head, especially if they represent societal norms.

- Don't let other people hijack your life.

    Be careful of people who want to tell you how to live your life. Honor yourself and fight to maintain your own dreams and aspirations,

- Don't overextend yourself in a competitive work scenario.

    Identify your personal level of comfort and acceptability with a challenging assignment and complete it to the best of your abilities and satisfaction.

Chapter Fourteen: Personal and Professional Passion and Flow

In this chapter we've decided to both focus on what factors cause people to have feelings of happiness, self-worth, job satisfaction and fulfilment. After some discussion (not all of it heated!) we've picked the elements of passion and flow to illustrate what exactly makes people feel invested in their work and personal life and what action precipitates it.

Elusive Happiness

Josh: A number of psychologists say that searching for happiness is useless and only results in the bitter taste of disappointment. I couldn't agree with them more. Chasing happiness is like chasing a rainbow. There it is, just beyond your reach, randomly appearing and disappearing, seducing you with its elusive beauty and promise of magic.

So if running after happiness won't actually make you happy, what will? I believe running toward what MAKES you happy might do the trick. What are you passionate about in life? When I ask this question, I'm not limiting it to what makes you passionately happy. Passion is an all-encompassing thing. It overarches happy and sad, good and bad; it is often two sides of the same coin.

What makes you passionately happy?

Passionately sad?

Passionately concerned?

Passionately interested?

Don't stop here. Make a list in your **Growth Games Workbook**. Review your answers. These are the things in life that make you feel ALIVE. Good and bad, happy or sad. These passions are what should get you up out of bed every morning and push you through each day until, exhausted you fall into a deep sleep so you can refuel and do it all over again the next day. Living your life through your passions is fulfilling, exciting, terrifying, challenging and satisfying. All of these feelings could also be attributed to successful personal and professional development.

Also, there is this thing called Flow. Flow, also known as "the zone", is the place you go mentally, when you are fully engaged in an activity, immersed in a state of energized focus, total investment and pure enjoyment. Hopefully you have had periods of Flow in your life. If you've experienced it once you'll never forget it. I believe when you live a life devoted to your passions and devote yourself 100 percent, you will start to achieve flow more and more consistently and this will herald the optimum state of continuous growth opportunity and development. If that isn't a recipe for happiness, I honestly don't know what is...

By Joshua Moore & Helen Glasgow

The Intrinsic Value of Work

Helen: I'm about to ask you two very personal questions, and that's not like me. But I need to know the answer and so do you. Why do you go to work? What do you get out of it? I know my answers, and I'm convinced because I do that's why I'm so good at what I do. I'm also equally convinced that lots of people go to work 8 plus hours a day, five days a week, 12 months a year, year in and year out, and don't know the honest to god answer to these questions. And that, my friends, is a real problem.

I've got more questions and I've made room for all of your answers in the **Growth Games workbook**. What is the value and pride you take from your job? Where do you see yourself when you envision your biggest professional success? What makes you passionate about your job? (Clue: if the answer to the passion question is "nothing" you need to dust off your resume. That's a big problem and honestly, you're devoting way too much of your life and energy to an activity that doesn't blow your socks off!)

Now about the Flow thing, or as I prefer to think of it, Being in the Zone.

You might be surprised but I'm a big fan of being in the zone. It's that same zone elite athletes talk about when they've finished first in a marathon or broken a world record or won their fourth gold medal. It's this place where all your preparation and training and passion and knowledge and talent and aspirations come together and Wham! You are in this state of absolute joy and power and self-fulfillment and no thing or person can touch you.

So find out what excites you professionally and then go out and be the best at it; keep the voices of your competition close enough to hear what they're saying, but don't let them get in your head. Keep your end goal, the #1 position in that pyramid in your sights at all time and don't stop until you touch it. And once you're there, don't forget to reach out and help the next guy get a little closer to his dreams. Don't worry – you'll be able to afford it.

The Big Takeaway:

After reviewing each other's advice and action steps for this chapter about passion and flow here are the 3 primary ideas we believe are the most integral to personal and/or professional growth:

- Identify your passions

    Good or bad, happy or sad, discover what you are passionate about in your personal and work life.

- Experience Flow

    Strive for that space where word and action come together in a zone of total investment and unadulterated bliss.

- Don't Settle

    If there is no passion or flow in your personal and/or professional life do something about it. Grow and develop until you find passion and flow and then grab onto it with your life!

Chapter Fifteen: To Thine Own Growth, Be True

In this chapter, we will get down to the business of developing individual personal and professional growth plans.

Putting it Together

Josh: The main problems I have with many personal and professional growth books and programs are twofold. First, although they are often very inspirational and offer a rich amount of theory, they tend to lose the plot when it comes to implementation. Second, there is often a "one size fits all" plan of attack. As we both have stressed over and over in this book, your individuality is one of your most powerful tools or gifts if the methods and actions of your growth implementation plan are chosen for YOU.

The following is a growth plan of action that addresses the concerns I've voiced above. I've included a full copy of this plan with enough space to make notes. You can also Xerox it and make multiple copies for future use.

Individualized Growth Plan of Action

What is your current Emotional Intelligence Position?

What is your main Personality Factor?

Who will be your Tribe?

Who will be your Reliable People?

What is your Inspirational Statement?

What is your Motivational Reward Statement?

What is/are your Aspirational Goal(s)?

What is your specific Plan of Attack to attain these goals, based on your Personality Factor and its strengths? (At least 3 activities should be included)

Make a daily calendar and find a way to incorporate one activity a day that is growth goal directed: (This only needs to take 15 or 20 minutes if you are busy or you can devote longer periods of time on days when you have more free time.)

What Social Skills will you incorporate in this action plan?

How will you Give Back during this process?

Describe how you envision your New Comfort Zone:

How will you incorporate Empathy in this action plan?

How will you incorporate your Passions in this growth process?

Selling Yourself as a BRAND

Helen: Wow Josh! Great job! That plan you wrote is comprehensive, detail-oriented and goal directed. If you substitute business terms such as co-pilots for reliable people and collaborators for tribes, it totally works for professional growth as well! I really only need to add one more element to this chapter.

In Business-speak, unique, individual development translates to creating your BRAND, as a professional and as an employee. Professional Branding is a fascinating topic and in all probability I will write a separate book on it at some point. For now, I want you to sit down, imagine yourself as your own boss and create the "Perfect Employee Brand" that s/he desires to supervise. How would you describe your strengths? How would they benefit the company? Which of your strengths is a "good fit" for this position? What would you want to be recognized for? (I've included these questions with room for answers in the **Growth Games workbook**)

There's a lot of buzz on the Internet about brand building, but only marketing professionals understand that if there is no point without brand promotion. In other words, if your "self-brand" remains only in your head no one will ever know about it!

Here are my two tips for self-brand promotion:

- Invest in yourself and TALK about it. You don't need to brag – keep it elegant and understated but get yourself out there.

- Make sure 3 groups of people have heard you, and now know about your self-investment. These groups can include: management, employees, horizontal-level colleagues and IDEALLY will include HR, clients/customers, if applicable and professionals in the industry.

Don't make that face! I am not suggesting you become some sleazy self-promotional bore that everybody hides from. Do you believe in yourself? Are you trying to be the best you can be as a business professional? What's sleazy about that?

Here's an example of graceful self-brand promotion:

Goal: You want to be known, or BRANDED for your newly improved and sharpened negotiation skills.

Graceful Self-Promotion: Casually mention a book you've recently read on the topic and recommend it to your colleagues. Piquing their curiosity, they will ask you about specific points and, as luck would have it, you can then SHARE your recent professional growth experience in the field of negotiations.

Graceful Self-Promotion: Mention to the boss that you recently spoke at a conference on negation – even if you just participated at a round table discussion.

Graceful Self-Promotion: Develop a small training on negotiation for your team and if you are confident enough, "allow" them to invite colleagues from another department, who will have to get permission from their bosses to attend, thus alerting said bosses to the fact you are an "expert" in negotiation!

How's that for grace under pressure?

The Big Takeaway:

After reviewing each other's advice and action steps for this chapter about implementing personal and professional growth development, here are the 3 primary ideas we believe are the most integral to personal and/or professional growth:

- Make a Growth Plan of Action

    Map out a concrete plan of action to ensure that your growth aspirations materialize into realized goals!

- Branding and Promotion

    Develop your plan to self-brand for professional growth development, and strategize how you can promote yourself in an elegant, graceful manner.

- READY. SET. GROW!!!

The Final Takeaway

One of our main objectives when writing this book was to offer ways to access and implement the many benefits of personal and professional growth to as wide and varied an audience as possible.

We guaranteed that this book would be different because we came from seemingly polar opposites of the personal and professional growth spectrum. When we set out to co-write this book we believed that our DIFFERENCES would offer fresh insight, new advice and novel approaches to the challenges of growth development. As we wrote, however, a fascinating transformation occurred. We found, as we delved deeper into the nuts and bolts of growth development and how to implement it personally and professionally, that we began to agree with each other more and more! We even, interestingly, began to adapt each other's advice and methodology until by the last chapter we had pretty much traded places! Josh offered a concrete Plan of Action, justifying every theoretical question with a definitive action-focused answer. Meanwhile, Helen was inviting her readers to "imagine that you are your boss"... and offering graceful and elegant ways to let your colleagues learn about your professional growth!

We are astounded and delighted with this result because by simply trusting our process, we unwittingly solved our big dilemma: How do you transfer or scaffold the benefits of personal growth to the professional work environment? It turns out, we both had some of the right answers and we couldn't be happier with our collective solutions. We hope you feel the same way.

If you haven´t done this already...

FREE DOWNLOAD

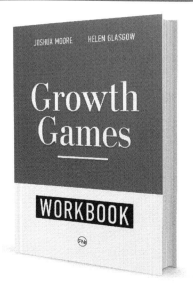

MAP YOUR GROWTH PLAN
STRAIGHT AWAY!

Sign up here to get a free copy of Growth Games
workbook and more:
www.frenchnumber.net/workbook

What Did You Think of Our Team Effort?

We've really enjoyed working on this book together and would appreciate your feedback!
So if you liked how we co-authored this book please let us know!

How you can do it:

1. **Review this book on Amazon**; just tell us what you liked the most and which key ideas you found the most useful

2. **Send us your feedback** here: growthreaders@gmail.com

Don't forget to mention which one of us you liked better (we have *a dinner bet* riding on this!)
Also, please feel free to tell us what other topics you'd like us to cover.

Yours,
Joshua and Helen

You may also like...
EMOTIONAL INTELLIGENCE SPECTRUM
EXPLORE YOUR EMOTIONS AND IMPROVE YOUR
INTRAPERSONAL INTELLIGENCE
BY JOSHUA MOORE AND HELEN GLASGOW

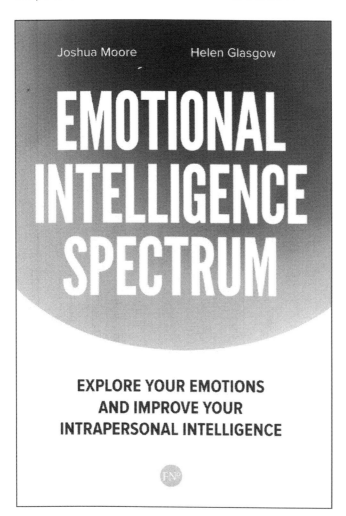

Emotional Intelligence Spectrum is the one book you need to buy if you've been curious about Emotional Intelligence, how it affects you personally, how to interpret EI in others and how to utilize Emotional Quotient in every aspect of your life.

Once you understand how EQ works, by taking a simple test, which is included in this guide, you will learn to harness the power of Emotional Intelligence and use it to further your career as you learn how to connect with people better.

You may also like...
I AM AN EMPATH
ENERGY HEALING GUIDE FOR EMPATHIC AND
HIGHLY SENSITIVE PEOPLE
BY JOSHUA MOORE

Am an Empath is an empathy guide on managing emotional anxiety, coping with being over emotional and using intuition to benefit from this sensitivity in your everyday life – the problems highly sensitive people normally face.

Through recongnizing how to control emotions you have the potential to make the most of being in tune with your emotions and understanding the feelings of people around you.
Begin your journey to a fulfilling life of awareness and support today!

You may also like...
MAKE ROOM FOR MINIMALISM
A PRACTICAL GUIDE TO SIMPLE AND
SUSTAINABLE LIVING
BY JOSHUA MOORE

By Joshua Moore & Helen Glasgow

Make Room for Minimalism is a clear cut yet powerful, step-by-step introduction to minimalism, a sustainable lifestyle that will enable you to finally clear away all the physical, mental and spiritual clutter that fills many of our current stress filled lives. Minimalism will help you redefine what is truly meaningful in your life.

Eager to experience the world of minimalism? Add a single copy of **Make Room for Minimalism** to your library now, and start counting the books you will no longer need!

FN№

Presented by French Number Publishing
French Number Publishing is an independent
publishing house headquartered in Paris, France
with offices in North America, Europe, and Asia.
FN№ is committed to connect the most promising
writers to readers from all around the world.
Together we aim to explore the most challenging
issues on a large variety of topics that are of
interest to the modern society.

FN№

By Joshua Moore & Helen Glasgow

Made in the USA
Columbia, SC
26 September 2018